To
Fr Cole,
a little part of
you is left behind,
because you tried to show
us Jesus more clearly.
Love & Peace Always
Mary

A Month with CHRIST

J. Murray Elwood

Ave Maria Press • Notre Dame, Indiana 46556

"It is with Christ that we journey and we walk with our steps in his footprints; he it is who is our guide and the burning flame which illumines our path; Pioneer of Salvation, it is he who draws us towards heaven, towards the Father, and promises success to those who seek him in faith. We shall one day be that which he is in glory if, by perfect imitation of his example here below, we become not mere Christians, but other Christs."

—St. Cyprian
Bishop of Carthage
and Martyr, 258 A.D.

For A. Robert Casey, friend and priest,
who has taught so many
the meaning of "Christ in My Heart."

Nihil Obstat:
Rev. J. Robert Yeazel
Censor Deputatus

Imprimatur:
Most Rev. Frank J. Harrison, D.D.
Bishop of Syracuse

International Standard Book Number: 0-87793-191-7 (cloth)
0-87793-192-5 (Paperback)

Library of Congress Catalog Card Number: 79-56214

Cover design and typography: Joyce Stanley

Printed and bound in the United States of America.

Contents

Introduction

Praying the Gospels

A gold-medal Olympic skier, recovering from a painful ankle injury, had no opportunity to practice on the slopes before an important race. The skier's only preparation was mental imagery. He pictured the downhill run in his imagination, skied it mentally beforehand and on the day of the real race went out to give one of the best performances of his career.

In a more familiar situation, a new business executive found herself feeling very uncomfortable when speaking in front of professional colleagues. An understanding counsellor taught the woman how to paint a positive mental picture beforehand. The executive was soon speaking more self-confidently because she had learned to think more positively of herself as a public speaker.

Mental training alone will never replace the need for skill and self-discipline, but it does seem to be a way that people can help themselves perform more effectively. It isn't only athletes who practice the "inner game" of golf or tennis, but musicians, ballet dancers — and also Christians.

The Christian "inner game" is known as meditation or mental prayer. It is a form of mental imagery which not only helps people to experience Jesus in a visual, real way but also enables them to copy his love and example in their daily lives.

Jesus once told his first followers, "I have given you an example that as I have done, so you do likewise" (Jn 13:15). "Learn from me," he said at another time, "for I am gentle and humble of heart" (Mt 11:29). St. Paul advised a group of early Christians, "Let this mind be in you which was also in Christ Jesus" (Phil 2:5), and he urged them to imitate the example of Christ in his self-surrendering love so that ". . . in our bodies the life of Jesus may also be revealed" (2 Cor 4:10). So Christians have always read the gospels, not only as a source of information about Jesus, but also as a guide for modelling their lives on the life of the Lord.

Meditation also offers another way in which the gospels are able to refresh the spirit of contemporary Christians. Jesus was once moving among a crowd of tightly packed people when a woman approached seeking a cure for a chronic illness. She heard about the Lord's healing power, but was too shy to approach him publicly for help; so she reached out and furtively touched the hem of his garment. "If I just touch his clothing," she thought, "I shall get well" (Mk 5:28). Power went out from the Lord and the woman was healed. After the cure Jesus explained to her, "Daughter, it is your faith that has cured you" (Mk 5:34).

Praying the gospels — meditating on the life of Jesus in scripture — is touching the hem of his garment; it is a special moment when power goes out from him. Christians believe that the Lord's power to heal is available in faith, not only to the original participants of any gospel event, but to all other believers who later approach those healing moments in prayerful memory.

Studying scripture, learning the reasons for religious belief, are necessary and important steps in the Christian life. There comes a time, however, if religion is to remain real, when men and women must go beyond studying Christ and begin experiencing him firsthand. "Christ in My Heart" is written for spiritual beginners. It is designed to help individuals and groups of new Christians grow from talking *about* Jesus to conversing *with* him, heart to heart.

Now most people, when they try to remember guitar chords or memorize formulas for a chemistry exam, discover that sometimes a little method will make a seemingly complicated task very easy. So it is with meditation. Praying the gospels becomes easy once beginners have learned to use a simple technique or method.

The form of prayer suggested by this book is one system of Christian meditation. There are many other ways to pray, but the method of "Christ in My Heart" has not only helped many people from all walks of life deepen their personal prayer, but it offers the extra advantages of being easy to remember, simple to use and central to the heart of all Christian life — the imitation of Christ in the gospels.

I. Preparing

Physical fitness enthusiasts, before they jog or play tennis, usually take a few minutes to limber up. Conditioning is important before any athletic effort, otherwise our bodies might find the sudden strain too much to bear. We'll pull a muscle or tear a tendon and then be unable to enjoy the sport.

Many failures at meditation occur because people forget that "warming up" is even more important for prayer than it is for tennis. So before beginning our conversation with the Lord it is necessary to take a few minutes to withdraw mentally from the bustle of the world around us, clear our minds of extraneous thoughts and prepare to enter his presence silently and reverently.

Sometimes it helps if we listen to the beating of our own heart for a few minutes or use the rhythm of our breathing as a way of turning inward. Consciously relaxing our muscles, repeating the Jesus Prayer or reciting a simple *mantra* are all forms of "centering" used by people as a preparation for prayer. We should use the form of "warming up" that works best for us, but we should never begin prayer without it.

II. Praying

Next we read very slowly a scene from the gospels — from the public life of Christ where the Lord is interacting with people in some special way. Then we enter that scene, copy the original experience and make it a springboard to prayer by following these three simple steps:

1. **Christ in My Eyes** — We paint a mental picture of the gospel scene in our imagination, not only visually, but with all our senses and feelings — in "living color." We are present as the event unfolds, we experience the scene as if it were actually happening. We hear the sounds of people's voices, see the reactions on different faces, push our way through a crowd of noisy bystanders and experience all the emotions caused by the original event. Who was there? What was said or done? How did Jesus respond? What do we feel? With the help of mental imagery, we begin our meditation by reliving the gospel scene as if we were experiencing it for the very first time.

2. **Christ in My Heart** — Then we reflect for a moment on the way Jesus spoke or acted in this gospel. We hear his words as if they were addressed to us: "You are anxious and upset about many things; one thing only is required." "Who do you say I am?" "It is I, do not be afraid." "Do you love me?" We answer him in our own way, with our own words. We tell him of our needs, our fears, our failures and our love.

We talk to Jesus as our best and dearest friend, from our heart.

Another way of starting our conversation with Christ is to role-play a gospel event in our imagination. We pretend that we are one of the participants in a certain New Testament scene and talk to him as if we were the man born blind, one of the ten lepers, Peter by the seashore, Mary Magdalene in the garden, or Thomas in the upper room. We begin by using the expressions these men and women in scripture spoke, then we continue our conversation with the Lord in our own way and with our own words.

We should spend as much time as we like in this part of our prayer. We share our lives with Jesus and rest in his love. We talk to him "heart to heart."

3. **Christ in My Hands** — The third step is to use our prayer to help us live more honest, more Christlike lives. So before finishing our meditation we ask ourselves how this gospel scene applies to real-life situations. What *one* thing will we do today — in our family, at work or on campus — to imitate Christ and really "live" this gospel? It is important that our choice aim at a specific step rather than a vague generality. Not, "I will be nicer today," but "I will tell my little sister I love her," or "I won't cut first class on Mondays," or "I'll come home early from the office and give the kids their baths tonight because my wife has evening class." Our decision should flow out of the gospel scene into a concrete action in our daily lives.

III. Prolonging

Finally, after each meditation there is a follow-up phrase for reflection — a few words or a line from scripture that is intended to be used as brief, spontaneous prayer for spare moments during the day — when walking between classes, for example, or riding home from work on the subway.

Just as the music of a television commercial reminds us of certain products, or a "golden-oldie" played on an FM station recalls persons from the past or some special moments in our lives, so the "follow-up" prayer is intended to lift our hearts to the Lord and recall our good resolutions to live the gospel in our daily lives.

Christ in My Heart is designed, in an easy, "do-it-yourself" format, to teach beginners how to pray. There are certain days, in the meditations that follow, when no gospel scene or prayer is written out so that the learner may be invited to develop his or her own prayer and practice, at first hand — the simple "Christ in My Heart" method. Like any new skill, prayer, for most people, doesn't just happen — it depends upon our success in setting aside a certain time each day when we sincerely try to learn how to pray.

"Prayer," St. Teresa once wrote, "consists not in much knowing, but in much loving." It is that treasure hidden in the field which is so spiritually beneficial and so humanly fulfilling that it is worth any effort we can make to uncover its riches. Nor will the Lord be blind to our attempts to learn the art of prayer. He will take pity upon our feeble efforts, even the most faltering steps taken in his direction, and he will reward us with that "pearl of great price" — the precious gift of prayer.

Beginnings 1

Christ in My Eyes

As he (Jesus) was walking along by the Sea of Galilee he saw Simon and his brother Andrew casting a net in the lake—for they were fishermen. And Jesus said to them, "Follow me and I will make you into fishers of men." And at once they left their nets and followed him.

Going on a little farther, he saw James son of Zebedee and his brother John; they too were in their boat, mending their nets. He called them at once and, leaving their father Zebedee in the boat with the men he employed, they went after him. Mk 1:16-20 (JB).

Our boat is moored by the shore. After sorting out last night's catch, I am now working in the bow with James and John. We are trying to mend our torn and tangled nets so that we may rejoin the other boats out on the lake. We have just about finished when we notice a man striding down the beach in our direction. It is the teacher, Jesus. His face is tanned, his manner self-assured; he is wearing a rough, white robe. Jesus stops a little way up the shoreline, calls across the water to Simon Peter's craft and continues on toward us. He approaches our boat, and beckons us with the same words, "Follow me!" In an instant, James and John drop their nets, jump over the side and splash up the shore after Jesus . . .

Christ in My Heart

Lord, your words were spoken first
to James and John,
but they were intended for me as well.
Yet here I am,
still sitting in the boat,
weighing my alternatives.
I wish I were as free
as these first followers—
just pack up, leave all things,
and put my past behind.
But I am so tied to my old ways,
so busy about worldly things,
that it isn't easy to cut loose,
leave everything,
and come along with you.
For you are really asking me
to risk my present happiness
for the sake of a future promise

on your word alone . . .
and I find that frightening.
But I am ready to try,
to take my first steps in your direction.
Be patient with a fainthearted disciple, Lord,
and help me to follow you.

Christ in My Hands

I will take time today to spend a few minutes alone with the Lord.

Reflect

"They went after him."

Following Christ 2

Christ in My Eyes

The next day John was there again with two of his disciples, when he saw Jesus walking by. "Here is the Lamb of God!" he said. The two disciples heard him say this and went with Jesus. Jesus turned, saw them following him, and asked, "What are you looking for?" They answered, "Where do you live, Rabbi?" (This word, translated, means "Teacher.") "Come and see," he answered. So they went with him and saw where he lived, and spent the rest of that day with him. (It was about four o'clock in the afternoon.) Jn 1:35-39.

We are walking along a sandy trail by a riverbank following a man in a long, white garment. He is only a short distance ahead, but seems unaware that we are trailing along behind. We are curious about this person, seem drawn to know more about him, but feel self-conscious and embarrassed about introducing ourselves. Suddenly the man senses our presence, looks back and, with a smile, asks us what we want. We hardly know how to answer, but blurt out awkwardly, "Where do you live, Rabbi?" Jesus replies warmly, "Come and see!"

Christ in My Heart

As I walk along this river path
I no longer feel uncomfortable and self-conscious
about meeting him.
Only very much at peace.
I tell him all about myself, confiding
my darkest fears and wildest dreams.
Somehow my mistakes in the past
and my wanderings in the present
do not bother me anymore.
The Lord knows the fickleness of my love,
but still invites me to be his friend. . .
Jesus, show me where you live.
Help me to experience you in my moments of prayer,
with all the enthusiasm
of meeting you for the very first time.
Show me where I may find you in the world about me.
And teach me how to prepare a daily place for you
in my heart.
"Where do you live, Lord?"

Christ in My Hands

I will set aside five extra minutes today to discover Jesus by reading scripture.

Reflect

"Come and see."

Burying the Past 3

Christ in My Eyes

As they went on their way, a certain man said to Jesus, "I will follow you wherever you go."

Jesus said to him, "Foxes have holes, and birds have nests, but the Son of Man has no place to lie down and rest." He said to another man, "Follow me."

But that man said, "Sir, first let me go back and bury my father."

Jesus answered, "Let the dead bury their own dead. You go and preach the Kingdom of God."

Another man said, "I will follow you, sir; but first let me go and say good-bye to my family."

Jesus said to him, "Anyone who starts to plow and then keeps looking back is of no use for the Kingdom of God."

Lk 9:57-62.

Along a road in Samaria, Jesus and the disciples are headed toward Jerusalem to worship at the great temple. A young man is standing by the roadside watching travellers as they pass. His wave is friendly and he appears so interested in the little group that Jesus walks over and invites him to join its company for the trip south. The youth, torn between his past and his future, hesitates a moment and then explains that he must bury his father first. Jesus' answer is uncompromising: "Let the dead bury their own dead. You go and preach the Kingdom of God."

Christ in My Heart

Jesus, so many "corpses" from my past
keep me from living in the present . . .
the real or imagined
failure of my parents,
or my early religious education
which I am still blaming for my unhappiness, even today.
My wallowings in the "what-might-have-been"
over lost loves
or missed opportunities.
My preoccupation with sins which God forgave so long ago,
but for which I have not yet forgiven myself.
Lord, call me away from
the graveyards of my past
and let the dead bury the dead
in my life.

Christ in My Hands

I will silently forgive someone who I feel has wronged or hurt me in the past.

Reflect

"Let the dead bury their own dead."

Priorities 4

Christ in My Eyes

As Jesus and his disciples went on their way, he came to a certain village where a woman named Martha welcomed him in her home. She had a sister named Mary, who sat down at the feet of the Lord and listened to his teaching. Martha was upset over all the work she had to do; so she came and said, "Lord, don't you care that my sister has left me to do all the work by myself? Tell her to come and help me!"

The Lord answered her, "Martha, Martha! You are worried and troubled over so many things, but just one is needed. Mary has chosen the right thing, and it will not be taken away from her." Lk 10:38-42.

Sunlight streams through the doorway of a small, one-room cottage. A kettle bubbles over the fire on an open hearth. Mary and I are seated at a wooden table listening to the Lord. I feel a deep peace sitting here with Jesus, but in the background there is the rattle of plates as Martha bustles around preparing supper. She pauses to stir the kettle, then looks over her shoulder reproachfully and interrupts our conversation, "Lord, tell my sister to help me!" "Martha," Jesus smiles, "you are worried and troubled over so many things, but just one is needed. . . ."

Christ in My Heart

Lord, you told us once that
people would only give their hearts
to what they really treasured.
Deep down,
what are the treasures
of my heart?
What do I usually daydream about
and where do I invest most of my emotional energies?
What am I most busy about—
  making money,
  escaping responsibilities,
  feeling sorry for myself,
  or resting in your love,
  putting my life in your hands?
I will tell you what I really want out of life.
I will ask your help to sift
the true from the false.
I listen
as you show me how to keep
first things first.

Christ in My Hands

Today, when I catch myself starting to worry or escaping by daydreams, I will put my life into the Lord's hands and go on living peacefully!

Reflect

"You are worried over so many things."

The Hungers of the Heart 5

Christ in My Eyes

Very early the next morning, long before daylight, Jesus got up and left the house. He went out of the town to a lonely place, where he prayed. But Simon and his companions went out searching for him; when they found him they said, "Everyone is looking for you."

But Jesus answered, "We must go on to the other villages around here. I have to preach in them also, because that is why I came." Mk 1:35-38.

Morning in Palestine

Long before daybreak, without waking any of us, Jesus quietly left the house where we were staying overnight and went off alone to a silent place to pray. Now Simon Peter and I, together with Andrew and John, walk out to the low hills beyond town looking for the Lord.

We find Jesus kneeling in a quiet olive grove, eyes closed, hands outstretched, his whole being absorbed in prayer. We feel drawn to share this wonderful experience, and forgetting for a moment the urgent needs in town, can only say, "Lord, teach us to pray."

Christ in My Heart

Lord, there is a stillness here
and a sense of peace
that make my life
and its problems
seem very far away.
I kneel close to you
in this olive grove
and as I see the inner calm
that floods your face,
I am overwhelmed
by my own poverty of spirit
and my desperate need
to draw close to the Father.
Help me to remember
the beauty of these special moments,
the sacred privilege of prayer . . .

I close my eyes, Lord,
put myself in the Father's presence,
and from the deep hunger
of my heart,
beg you,
"Lord, teach me how to pray."

Christ in My Hands

No matter how busy my day, I will make space for reflective silence.

Reflect

"He went out of the town to a lonely place, where he prayed."

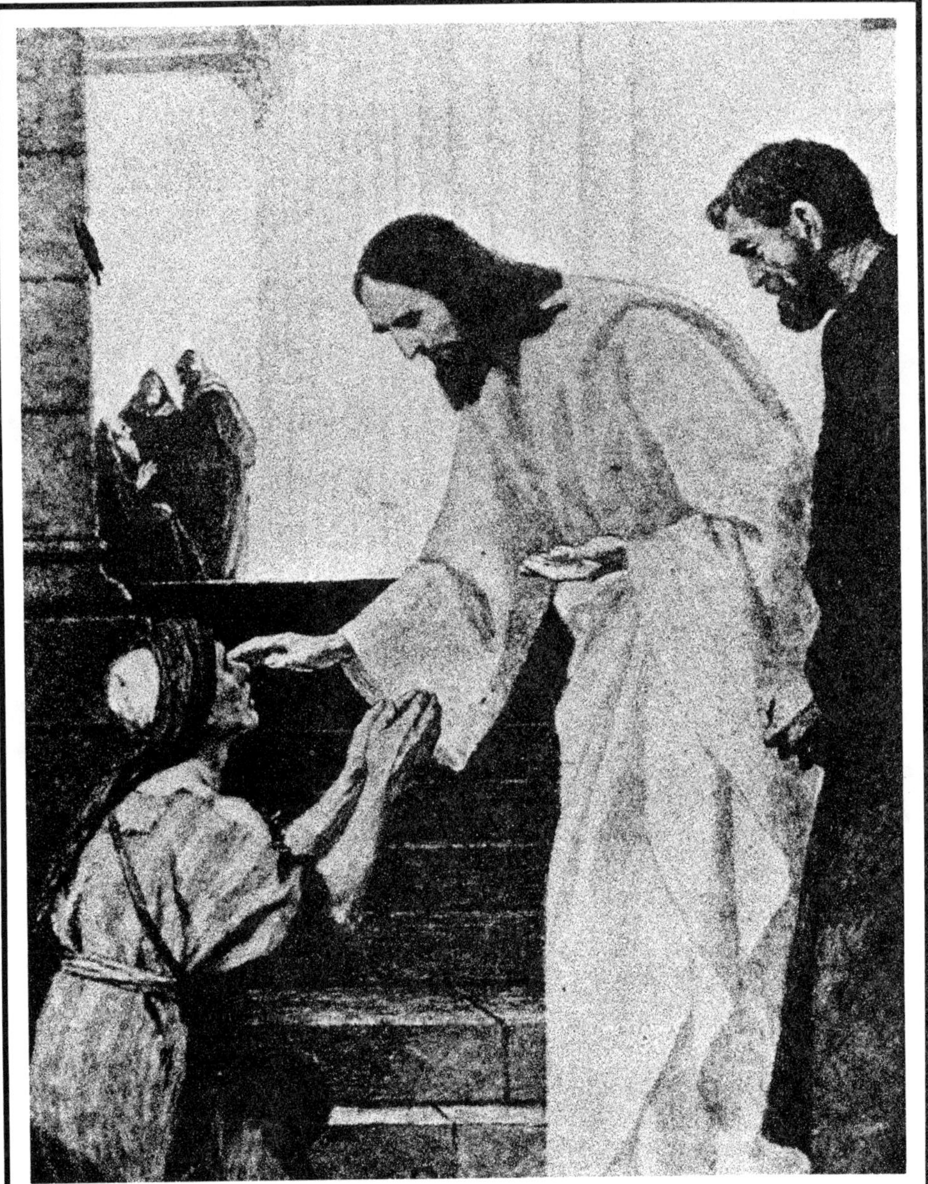

6 Facing Reality

Christ in My Eyes

They came to Jericho. As Jesus was leaving with his disciples and a large crowd, a blind man named Bartimaeus, the son of Timaeus, was sitting by the road, begging.

When he heard that it was Jesus of Nazareth, he began to shout, "Jesus! Son of David! Have mercy on me!"

Many scolded him and told him to be quiet. But he shouted even more loudly, "Son of David, have mercy on me!"

Jesus stopped and said, "Call him."

So they called the blind man. "Cheer up!" they said "Get up, he is calling you."

He threw off his cloak, jumped up and came to Jesus.

"What do you want me to do for you?" Jesus asked him.

"Teacher," the blind man answered, "I want to see again."

"Go," Jesus told him, "your faith has made you well."

At once he was able to see, and followed Jesus on the road.
Mk 10:46-52.

Sitting by the side of the road on a warm, sweltering day, I feel sweaty and helpless. My blind eyes see only blackness, but in the distance I hear the shuffle of an approaching crowd. Then I am confused by the sound of many voices. My hands clutch at a bystander. "What is happening?" I ask. A man in the crowd answers that Jesus of Nazareth is passing by. Suddenly I start shouting, "Son of David, have mercy on me. . . ! Son of David, hear me!" "He's calling you," someone whispers in my ear. I am pulled to my feet and am pushed forward. Two strong hands grasp my shoulders. "What do you want me to do for you?" a deep voice asks. "Lord," I beg, "I want to see. . . .I want to see!"

Christ in My Heart

Lord, sometimes my eyes are closed
and I am as blind to life around me
as the beggar in the gospel.
There is so much that I am afraid to see,
so many things I am unwilling to face —
  my rationalizations,
  my insensitivity to others' feelings,
  my constant self-criticism,
  my negative thinking,
  my self-destructive behaviors,
  my dependency relationships,
  my delusions and false views of life.
Lord, I am blind.
Open my eyes that I may see.
Help me to face whatever I am avoiding.
Lord, I want to see!

Christ in My Hands

I will face one task today I have avoided all week.

Reflect

"Lord, I want to see!"

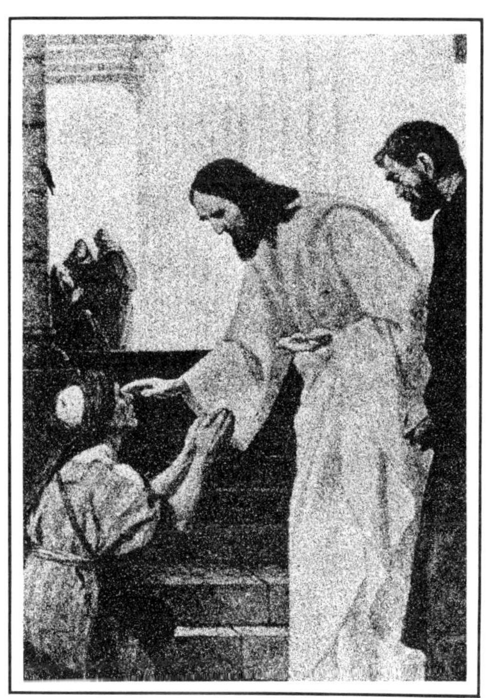

7 Life's Storms

Christ in My Eyes

On the evening of that same day Jesus said to his disciples, "Let us go across to the other side of the lake."

So they left the crowd; the disciples got into the boat that Jesus was already in, and took him with them. Other boats were there too. A very strong wind blew up and the waves began to spill over into the boat, so that it was about to fill with water. Jesus was in the back of the boat, sleeping with his head on a pillow. The disciples woke him up and said, "Teacher, don't you care that we are about to die?" Jesus got up and commanded the wind: "Be quiet!" and said to the waves, "Be still!" The wind died down, and there was a great calm. Then Jesus said to them, "Why are you frightened? Are you still without faith?" But they were terribly afraid, and began to say to each other, "Who is this man? Even the wind and the waves obey him!" Mk 4:35-41.

Huge waves break against the side of our leaking boat and the torn sail snaps wildly in the wind. The water slowly filling our small craft is up to my ankles; my arms ache from our frantic bailing, but nothing seems to help. The wind grows stronger and the waves keep getting higher. I expect that we will capsize at any moment. From the look on his face and the way he clutches the side of the boat, I can tell that Peter is badly frightened, too. Jesus is the only one not bothered by the storm — he sleeps peacefully on a cushion in back. But we are desperate, so in panic I shake Jesus' shoulder. "Save us, Lord," we shout above the roar of the wind, "we're going to die!" Suddenly there is a great silence. The sea is calm, the winds die down. "Why are you so frightened?" Jesus asks, then he complains, "What little faith you have!"

Christ in My Heart

Lord,
how have I reacted to the sudden, unexpected
storms in my life?
  the loss of a job
  breaking up with someone I loved,
  an unplanned pregnancy,
  failing a required course,
  the sudden death of a parent or friend.
Didn't I panic,
like the disciples in the leaky boat,
and forget your presence in my life?
Am I the kind of Christian
who needs your constant attention and reassurance,
or can I trust in your loving care
for me,
even when your silence sounds like
you are sleeping?

Christ in My Hands

I will tell Jesus that I trust him to calm the secret storm in my life whenever and in whatever way he thinks best.

Reflect

"Why are you frightened?"

Staying 8

Christ in My Eyes

Jesus said to them: "I tell you the truth: if you do not eat the flesh of the Son of Man and drink his blood you will not have life in yourselves. Whoever eats my flesh and drinks my blood has eternal life, and I will raise him to life on the last day. For my flesh is the real food, my blood is the real drink. Whoever eats my flesh and drinks my blood lives in me and I live in him. The living Father sent me, and because of him I live also. In the same way, whoever eats me will live because of me.

"This, then, is the bread that came down from heaven; it is not like the bread that your ancestors ate and then died. The one who eats this bread will live for ever." Jesus said this as he taught in the synagogue in Capernaum.

Many of his disciples heard this and said, "This teaching is too hard. Who can listen to this?"

Because of this, many of his followers turned back and would not go with him any more. So Jesus said to the twelve disciples, "And you — would you like to leave also?" Simon Peter answered him: "Lord, to whom would we go? You have the words that give eternal life. And now we believe and know that you are the Holy One from God" Jn 6:53-60,66-70.

Inside the small synagogue at Capernaum, men sit on benches along one side of the whitewashed walls, women on the other. After the opening prayer and a reading from the Law and the Prophets, Jesus is invited to give the homily. He moves to the middle of the room and speaks earnestly about feeding people in a new way, with a bread that comes down from heaven. Many people in the congregation shake their heads in disbelief, others whisper angrily among themselves. Some get up and walk out. Jesus comes over to where the disciples and I are seated, searches our faces for a moment, then asks softly, "Would you like to leave also?" "To whom would we go, Lord?" Peter asks. "You have the words that give eternal life!"

Christ in My Heart

Lord,
there are no windows
into other people's souls,
no one's motives to judge
except my own.
But some days it seems as if
the whole world is turning
away from you.
So many of my friends,
even members of my own family,
no longer share your Eucharistic bread,
no longer walk in your company.
Jesus, you want my love,
but you respect my freedom,
so you ask,
"Would you like to leave also?"
Sometimes I don't know the reasons why I stay
when so many others walk away —
only that I would miss you.

That my heart would be empty
without you.
So with Peter's words,
and in my own way, I say,
"To whom would I go?
Only you have the words
of eternal life!"

Christ in My Hands

The next time I hear the church criticized, I will show my gratitude for my religious family by speaking up to defend the Christian community.

Reflect

"Would you like to leave also?"

Responsibility 9

Christ in My Eyes

"It will be like a man who was about to leave home on a trip; he called his servants and put them in charge of his property. He gave to each one according to his ability: to one he gave five thousand dollars, to the other two thousand dollars, and to the other one thousand dollars. Then he left on his trip. . . .

"After a long time the master of those servants came back and settled accounts with them. The servant who had received five thousand dollars came in and handed over the other five thousand dollars. 'You gave me five thousand dollars, sir,' he said. 'Look! Here are another five thousand dollars that I have earned.' 'Well done, good and faithful servant!' said his master. 'You have been faithful in managing small amounts, so I will put you in charge of large amounts. Come on in and share my happiness!' Then the servant who had been given two thousand dollars came in and said, 'You gave me two thousand dollars, sir. Look! Here are another two thousand dollars that I have earned.' 'Well done, good and faithful servant!' said his master. 'You have been faithful in managing small amounts, so I will put you in charge of large amounts. Come on in and share my happiness!' "
Mt 25: 14-15,19-23.

The deep blue of the sky, the warmth of the sunshine and the call of birds on the wing — all these images help me picture a beautiful spring morning. The apostles and I are walking with Jesus along a path headed south towards Jerusalem. The Lord's gestures are expansive, and his face lights up as he tells us a wonderful story about the use of God's gifts in our lives. "Invest this until I return," Jesus has the nobleman say in St. Luke's retelling of the story and by these words he implies that I shouldn't be afraid of running risks, and that the Lord trusts me with my talents; he wants me to make choices and invest his gifts as I think best.

Christ in My Heart

Lord, you have left me in this world
with my abilities and special skills.
Like the nobleman,
you go away for a while,
but ask me to invest them
until you return.
So I am free to make choices
about the way
I will use these talents.
This gives me a great feeling
of peace, Lord,
just thinking about my possibilities
and your great trust in me.
But free choice is also frightening
and at times I'm awfully tempted
to play it safe —
to put your treasures on the shelf,
or bury them in the ground.
You have trusted me, Lord,
now help me to trust myself.

May I stand on my own two feet,
be less fearful of taking risks
and more free in using those talents
you have placed in my hands.

Christ in My Hands

I will make a decision today that I have been putting off.

Reflect

"Invest until I return!"

Forgiveness 10

Christ in My Eyes

Jesus spoke up and said to him, "Simon, I have something to tell you."

"Yes, Teacher," he said, "tell me."

"There were two men who owed money to a moneylender," Jesus began; "one owed him five hundred dollars and the other one fifty dollars. Neither one could pay him back, so he canceled the debts of both. Which one, then, will love him more?"

"I suppose," answered Simon, "that it would be the one who was forgiven more."

"Your answer is correct," said Jesus. Then he turned to the woman and said to Simon, "Do you see this woman? I came into your home, and you gave me no water for my feet, but she has washed my feet with her tears and dried them with her hair. You did not welcome me with a kiss, but she has not stopped kissing my feet since I came. You provided no oil for my head, but she has covered my feet with perfume. I tell you, then, the great love she has shown proves that her many sins have been forgiven. Whoever has been forgiven little, however, shows only a little love."

Then Jesus said to the woman, "Your sins are forgiven."
Lk 7:40-48.

Oil lamps along the walls cast a flickering light on the well-laden dinner table in Simon's home.

About a dozen men, prominent citizens in the town, lie on divans around the table. Jesus, as guest of honor, reclines on the couch next to Simon's, but the atmosphere at the meal, while proper, is not friendly. I notice Simon and his friends watching Jesus very closely.

Suddenly, a door leading to the street opens and a tall, attractive woman enters the room. She is not wearing a veil and is carrying a small white jar. The woman glances around quickly, sees where Jesus is reclining and goes over to kneel at the foot of his couch. She kisses his feet and begins to cry; then she empties the contents of the jar, unloosens a ribbon and begins drying his feet with her hair. The dining room grows very quiet, the other guests are shocked by the woman's behavior. Jesus speaks softly and uses the occasion to teach a lesson about God's mercy. "The great love she has shown," Jesus says of the woman, "proves that her many sins have been forgiven."

Christ in My Heart

Lord, today I imagine
that I'm the woman
who interrupted Simon's dinner party.
Why did I enter this private home,
kneel beside a couch
and begin washing your feet?
Was I trying to make up
for the discourteous way
you were being treated,
or did I just react,
overwhelmed by my need
to be near you?
I brought a jar of perfume
and my tears.

I want to lay at your feet —
  my confusions about life,
  the conflicts I feel,
  the pain I have caused those I love.
And I also want to say
that I am sorry
for my failures in the past,
especially when I have wavered
in my love for you.
Jesus, in the warmth of your love,
my mistakes seem
like a small drop of water
in a blazing fire.
I tell you that I am sorry.
Take my sins
and speak to me again
your forgiving words of love.

Christ in My Hands

I will eliminate from my life one thing that is holding me back from a closer union with the Lord.

Reflect

"The great love she has shown proves her many sins have been forgiven."

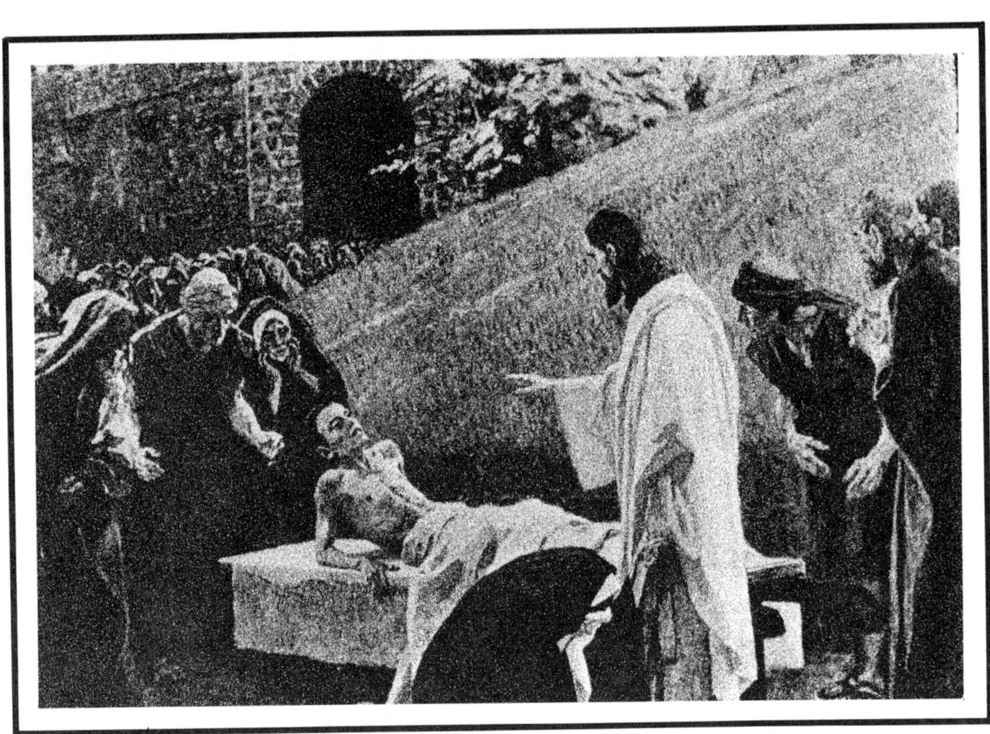

Compassion 11

Christ in My Eyes

Soon afterward Jesus went to a town named Naim; his disciples and a large crowd went with him. Just as he arrived at the gate of the town, a funeral procession was coming out. The dead man was the only son of a woman who was a widow, and a large crowd from the city was with her. When the Lord saw her his heart was filled with pity for her and he said to her, "Don't cry." Then he walked over and touched the coffin, and the men carrying it stopped. Jesus said, "Young man! Get up, I tell you!" The dead man sat up and began to talk, and Jesus gave him back to his mother.

Everyone was filled with fear, and they praised God, "A great prophet has appeared among us!" and, "God has come to save his people!" Lk 7:11-16.

Springtime in Galilee.

The morning air is fresh and clean. I have been travelling down the road from Capernaum with the apostles and the Lord. Jesus leads the way and we follow in groups of two and three.

As we approach the walls of a small town we notice a commotion on the road ahead. Coming out of the main gate is a long funeral procession. A woman, leaning on the arms of friends, is in front and she is followed by two men who carry the body of a young man on a stretcher. His limbs are stiff, his flesh gray and his face is covered by a linen cloth.

Jesus looks sadly at the weeping woman, takes her by the hand and whispers gently, "Don't cry." Then he touches the stretcher and loudly commands, "Young man, I tell you, get up!" The corpse begins to move, color slowly returns to the extremities, and the young man, looking very bewildered, starts to sit up. All of us stare speechlessly as the Lord gives the son back to his mother.

Christ in My Heart

Jesus, it is a great miracle
to raise a man from the dead.
But what moves me most
about this scene
is Luke's observation
that at this poor woman's pain,
your heart was "filled with pity."
So as I stand here by the dead man's stretcher,
I do not so much ask for signs and wonders,
for great miracles of healing,
or even that the dead should rise,
only that you will still take pity
on the pain of the human condition,
on those who walk life's way

burdened with loneliness or loss.
Raise us at the last day,
dry forever our tears
and give us back to each other
as you once returned the son to the widow.

Christ in My Hands

I will be especially sensitive to those who have lost someone they love.

Reflect

"When the Lord saw her, his heart was filled with pity. . . ."

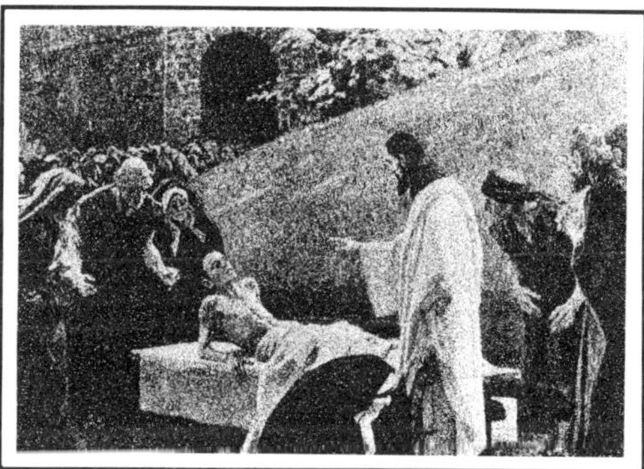

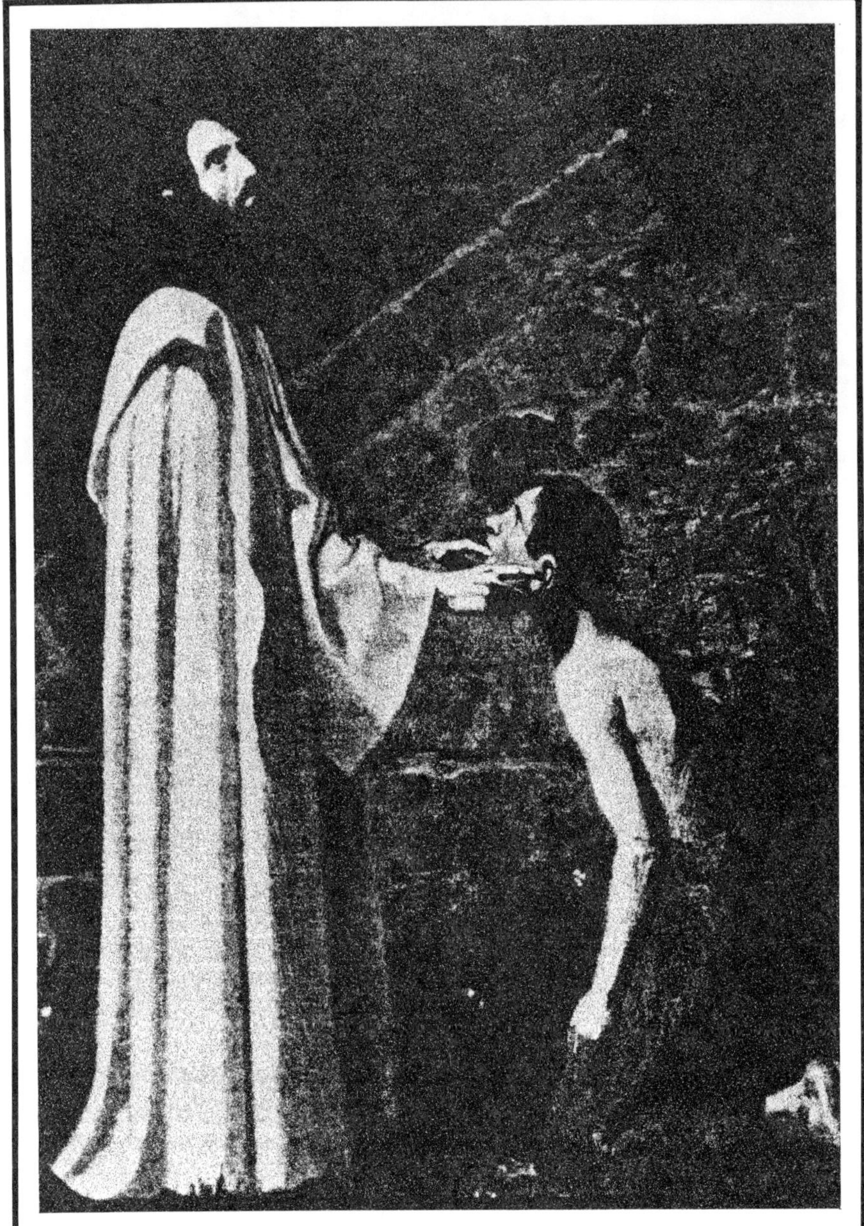

Speech Impediments 12

Christ in My Eyes

Jesus then left the neighborhood of Tyre and went on through Sidon to Lake Galilee, going by way of the territory of the Ten Towns. Some people brought him a man who was deaf and could hardly speak, and begged Jesus to place his hand on him. So Jesus took him off alone, away from the crowd, put his fingers in the man's ears, spat, and touched the man's tongue. Then Jesus looked up to heaven, gave a deep groan, and said to the man, Ephphatha, *which means, "Open up!" At once the man's ears were opened, his tongue was set loose, and he began to talk without any trouble. Then Jesus ordered them all not to speak of it to anyone; but the more he ordered them, the more they told it. And all who heard were completely amazed. "How well he does everything!" they exclaimed. "He even makes the deaf to hear and the dumb to speak!"* Mk 7:31-37.

We are in pagan territory, beyond the Jordan, on the eastern side of the Sea of Galilee. The Lord has been travelling through towns and villages preaching the kingdom of God and healing all kinds of infirmities. Word of Jesus' presence has spread through the whole district so that the crowds of people who come running out of the villages to meet us have grown larger every day.

This afternoon, as we round a bend in the road, a large group of men and women stand across our path waiting for Jesus to pass by. When they see the Lord, the crowd pushes a man from their village forward and begs Jesus to heal him. The man's eyes have a vacant stare, his mouth hangs open and he makes unintelligible sounds as he shuffles up to Jesus. The Lord takes the deaf-mute to the side of the road, a little apart from the crowd, and puts his fingers in the man's ears. Then he touches his tongue-tied mouth saying softly, "Be opened!" A look of surprise crosses the man's face, his eyes focus on Jesus and he begins to speak coherently.

Christ in My Heart

Lord, it almost seems
that this scene was written just for me. . . .
I need no special skills
to role-play this part,
for you know
how insensitive I am,
how often I do not understand
the needs or the pain of those around me.
Nor do I even listen
to my own conscience,
the sound of your voice within.
And those words which should comfort —
   the warm words,
   the tender words,
   the kind words,

the words which say I care,
are all distorted
or never spoken.
Open my ears,
loosen my tongue
that I may hear those voices,
praise your name
and speak more of your love to others.

Christ in My Hands

I will make an effort today, in my casual conversations, to listen more carefully and speak more lovingly.

Reflect

"He even makes the deaf to hear and the dumb to speak!"

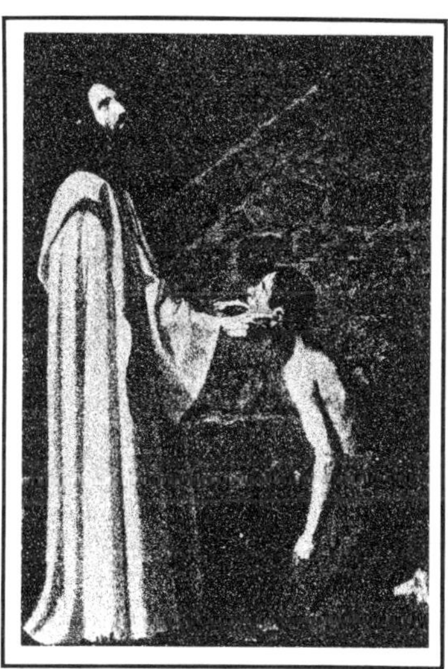

Touching Jesus 13

Christ in My Eyes

As Jesus went along, the people were crowding him from every side. A certain woman was there who had suffered from severe bleeding for twelve years; she had spent all she had on doctors, but no one had been able to cure her. She came up in the crowd behind Jesus and touched the edge of his cloak, and her bleeding stopped at once. Jesus asked, "Who touched me?"

Everyone denied it, and Peter said, "Master, the people are all around you and crowding in on you."

But Jesus said, "Someone touched me, for I knew it when power went out of me." The woman saw that she had been found out, so she came, trembling, and threw herself at Jesus' feet. There, in front of everybody, she told him why she had touched him and how she had been healed at once. Jesus said to her, "My daughter, your faith has made you well. Go in peace." Lk 8:42-48.

The mob of people waiting on the beach starts running in our direction even before we reach shore. No sooner do we step out of our little boat than the apostles and I are swallowed up by this swirling mass of humanity.

Jesus slowly pushes his way through the crowd and we try to follow. I am right behind the Lord when a woman jostles me out of the way and clutches at the fringe of his cloak.

Instantly, Jesus stops and, looking back at us, asks, "Who touched me?" Peter explains that the crowd is so large that everyone is touching him, but Jesus in insistent. "I knew it when power went out of me," he says. The woman, now trembling all over, kneels at the Lord's feet and hesitantly explains that her sickness has been healed. "Your faith has made you well," answers Jesus. "Go in peace."

Christ in My Heart

Lord, you once said
that only the violent
could storm heaven's gates.
So this woman's determination,
despite all obstacles to resist
the pressure of the crowd
and persevere in her good intentions,
is rewarded
when at last she is able
to touch the hem of the garment
and experience
your healing power.
Jesus, my own efforts
to follow you
seem feeble by comparison.
My intentions are sincere,
but my steps so often falter

if they are not encouraged
by those around me.
Free me from my dependence
on other people's approval.
Help me to persevere
in my own attempts
to come close to you.

Christ in My Hands

I will receive the sacrament of reconciliation whenever I feel the need.

Reflect

"Your faith has made you well. Go in peace."

Leprosy 

Christ in My Eyes

Once Jesus was in a certain town where there was a man who was covered with leprosy. When he saw Jesus, he threw himself down and begged him, "Sir, if you want to, you can make me clean!"

Jesus reached out and touched him. "I do want to," he answered. "Be clean!" At once the leprosy left the man. Jesus ordered him, "Don't tell this to anyone, but go straight to the priest and let him examine you; then offer the sacrifice, as Moses ordered, to prove to everyone that you are now clean." Lk 5:12-14.

Barking dogs follow a man limping down the main street of a Galilean town. Shreds of rotten bandages hang from his hands and feet and his swollen face is disfigured with the advanced stages of disease. Bystanders shrink away while mothers pull their children out of the man's path. He is a leper and, in open violation of Jewish law, has dared to enter this town to find Jesus.

Suddenly, the leper notices the Lord standing at the far end of the street. He cries out and hobbles over to fall at Jesus' feet. "Sir, if you want to, you can make me clean," he begs. The Lord's hand touches the man's infected body. "I do want to," he replies. "Be clean!" says the Lord.

Christ in My Heart

Jesus, today I wear the leper's rags.
My body stinks with putrid sores
and I am weak with the fever
of my disease.
But what hurts most
is the loneliness and isolation
living outside of town
and cut off from those I love.
Lord, what sort of deformities
isolate me today
from those around me?
Is it my judgmental attitude —
  my mistrust of people's motives,
  my need always to have the last word,
  to act superior, to play games,
  or my unwillingness
  to give others the benefit of the doubt?
The list is long
and only you can help me see

what isolates me from other people.
Heal my wounds,
help me to be a more complete person.
If you want to, Lord,
you can make me clean!

Christ in My Hands

I will ask my best friend for an honest estimate of my worst verbal game or most annoying behavior.

Reflect

"He fell on his face before him and begged."

Self-Acceptance 15

Read the following gospel passage and write your own meditation.

Christ in My Eyes

One time Jesus was standing on the shore of Lake Gennesaret while the people pushed their way up to him to listen to the word of God. He saw two boats pulled up on the beach; the fishermen had left them and were washing the nets. Jesus got into one of the boats—it belonged to Simon—and asked him to push off a little from the shore. Jesus sat in the boat and taught the crowd.

When he finished speaking, he said to Simon, "Push the boat out further to the deep water, and you and your partners let your nets down for a catch."

"Master," Simon answered, "we worked hard all night long and caught nothing. But if you say so, I will let down the nets." They let the nets down and caught such a large number of fish that the nets were about to break. So they motioned to their partners in the other boat to come and help them. They came and filled both boats so full of fish that they were about to sink. When Simon Peter saw what had happened, he fell on his knees before Jesus and said, "Go away from me, Lord! I am a sinful man!"
Lk 5:1-8.

Describe this scene in your own words.

Christ in My Heart

Write out a conversation with the Lord based on this gospel.

Christ in My Hands

What is a practical application of this gospel to your daily life?

Reflect

A line from scripture to recall your prayer.

Sincerity 16

Christ in My Eyes

"It is not those who say to me, 'Lord, Lord,' who will enter the kingdom of heaven, but the person who does the will of my Father in heaven. When the day comes many will say to me, 'Lord, Lord, did we not prophesy in your name, cast out demons in your name, work many miracles in your name?' Then I shall tell them to their faces: I have never known you; away from me, you evil men!

"Therefore, everyone who listens to these words of mine and acts on them will be like a sensible man who built his house on rock. Rain came down, floods rose, gales blew and hurled themselves against that house, and it did not fall: it was founded on rock. But everyone who listens to these words of mine and does not act on them will be like a stupid man who built his house on sand. Rain came down, floods rose, gales blew and struck that house, and it fell; and what a fall it had!" Mt 7:21-27 (JB).

The morning sun sparkles on the blue water as I walk by the Sea of Galilee. Many other people are on the beach this morning, all hurrying along toward a fishing boat moored a short distance offshore. Jesus is seated in the bow of the small craft and his smile is warm and welcoming. A large number of people are reclining on the sandy shore, but I am able to find a place quite close to the boat. I, too, sit on the sand and listen to the Lord as he begins to speak.

Jesus' voice carries over the still waters and he talks to us kindly but firmly about sincerity in religion and the need for people to link their faith with their daily lives. I see the earnest expression on his face, hear the forceful ways in which he makes his point. I begin to reflect upon my own life and the way I practice my faith.

Christ in My Heart

Jesus, sometimes religion has been described as
"the opium of the people."
The phrase suggests that something
even as sacred as prayer
can be an escape from reality
when it does not relate to daily life.
I praise you with my lips
and rejoice to call you Lord,
but my worship must be more than words.
You remind us in so many ways that
true devotion flows into deeds —
welcoming strangers,
healing the brokenhearted,
caring for the sick,
housing the homeless,
feeding the hungry.
Lord, help me to act upon your words.

And in these moments of prayer
when I feel very close to you,
keep reminding me that discipleship means ministering
to the needs of others.

Christ in My Hands

I will take time to visit a sick friend or relative in the hospital.

Reflect

"It is not those who say to me, 'Lord, Lord,' who will enter the kingdom of heaven, but the person who does the will of my Father in heaven."

Caring 17

Christ in My Eyes

But the teacher of the Law wanted to put himself in the right, so he asked Jesus, "Who is my fellow-man?"

Jesus answered, "There was a man who was going down from Jerusalem to Jericho, when robbers attacked him, stripped him, and beat him up, leaving him half dead. It so happened that a priest was going down that road; when he saw the man he walked on by, on the other side. In the same way a Levite also came there, went over and looked at the man, and then walked on by, on the other side. But a certain Samaritan who was traveling that way came upon him, and when he saw the man his heart was filled with pity. He went over to him poured oil and wine on his wounds and bandaged them; then he put the man on his own animal and took him to an inn, where he took care of him. The next day he took out two silver coins and gave them to the innkeeper. 'Take care of him,' he told the innkeeper, 'and when I come back this way I will pay you back whatever you spend on him.' "

And Jesus concluded, "In your opinion, which one of these three acted like a fellow-man toward the man attacked by the robbers?"

The teacher of the Law answered, "The one who was kind to him."

Jesus replied, "You go, then, and do the same." Lk 10:29-37.

The mood of the crowd surrounding Jesus is hostile. Pharisees and teachers of the law have gathered from many different parts of Galilee and Judea to hear this new Rabbi and, if possible, trap him in his teaching. Some in the Lord's audience shake their heads in disbelief at what he says; others are visibly impressed and listen with reverent attention. Despite the tightly packed throng surrounding the Lord, I am able to squeeze quite close and hear him answering the crowd's questions in his clear, strong voice.

Suddenly a lawyer, anxious to impress his colleagues and discredit Jesus, asks some seemingly simple questions about his religious duties. Jesus replies by relating the story of the traveller, mugged by robbers, who was befriended by a kind Samaritan. The Lord concludes his story by commanding the lawyer, "You go, then, and do the same!"

Christ in My Heart

Lord, how many men and women
do I meet
who are victims by the roadside of life?
How many people,
through no fault of their own,
have been robbed of their precious birthright
for full human and spiritual growth?
They are all around me, these wounded persons—
   an alcoholic parent,
   a forgotten senior citizen,
   a socially inadequate roommate,
   an abandoned wife.

But like the priest and Levite in your story,
I am often tempted not to get involved,
to pass my battered brothers and sisters by.
Teach me, by the example of the Good Samaritan,

how I, too, can become a healer
by pouring into the wounds
of those who have fallen by life's wayside
the oil and wine of love and kindness.
Lord, help me heal the brokenhearted.

Christ in My Hands

I will be more sensitive to the lonely people in my life.

Reflect

"His heart was filled with pity."

Mountains and Valleys 18

Christ in My Eyes

Six days later Jesus took Peter, James, and John with him, and led them up a high mountain by themselves. As they looked on, a change came over him, and his clothes became shining white, whiter than anyone in the world could wash them. Then the three disciples saw Elijah and Moses, who were talking with Jesus. Peter spoke up and said to Jesus, "Teacher, it is a good thing that we are here. We will make three tents, one for you, one for Moses, and one for Elijah." He and the others were so frightened that he did not know what to say.

A cloud appeared and covered them with its shadow, and a voice came from the cloud, "This is my own dear Son—listen to him!" They took a quick look around but did not see anyone else; only Jesus was with them.

As they came down the mountain Jesus ordered them, "Don't tell anyone what you have seen, until the Son of Man has risen from death." Mk 9:2-9.

We have been climbing all morning and have finally reached a flat, windy space near the top of a mountain. The view is spectacular. On all sides the horizon stretches off into the distance, and to the south we can make out the Sea of Galilee and the Jordan valley beyond. Jesus withdraws a short distance to pray, while the three apostles and I begin to doze after our exhausting climb.

Suddenly, we are jolted awake by a strange event. Jesus' appearance has changed — his face glows and the brightness of his clothes hurts our eyes. Two ghostly figures, Moses and Elijah, appear beside him. At first we tremble with fright, but this soon gives way to an overwhelming feeling of happiness and peace. Life's problems seem so far removed from this mountain that the apostles and I could pitch tents here and stay forever. "Teacher," we blurt out, hardly knowing what to say, "it is a good thing that we are here!"

Christ in My Heart

Jesus, with the pressures and tensions
of life's daily trials,
I guess it is only natural
to feel so overwhelmed
by the happiness and joy
I experience with you on this mountaintop .
I think of the peak experiences in my own life —
  a really good confession,
  the fellowship of a prayer group,
  an Encounter weekend,
  a school retreat,
  or just some special moment
  with my friends.
It was good for me to be here.

And I thank you
  for such special moments of grace . . .
  all those times
  when I felt close to you
  on my very own mountain.
But you wouldn't let the apostles
stay on their mountain.
  You led them down
  into the valleys of life.
Lord, I am grateful for my mountaintop days,
but they are special gifts,
rare tokens of your love for me.
Help me to persevere
  in the ordinary ways,
  among the shadows in the valley,
where love is shown,
not by great bursts of feeling,
but by fidelity
in the daily tasks of living.

Christ in My Hands

I will be contented with the routine of my life today.

Reflect

"This is my own dear Son — listen to him!"

Simplicity 19

Christ in My Eyes

Some people brought children to Jesus for him to touch them, but the disciples scolded those people. When Jesus noticed it, he was angry and said to his disciples, "Let the children come to me, and do not stop them, because the Kingdom of God belongs to such as these. Remember this! Whoever does not receive the Kingdom of God like a child will never enter it." Then he took the children in his arms, placed his hands on each of them, and blessed them. Mk 10:13-16.

Inside a home where Jesus is teaching.

Men from the village have pushed their way into the small room and I am now seated with them on the dirt floor listening to the Lord's words. A commotion at the doorway announces some women who are trying to enter the house with their children. Peter blocks their way explaining that there is no more room, but the women keep insisting that they want Jesus to bless their babies. When the Lord notices their presence, he is angry with Peter and clears a way through the crowded room for the mothers and their children. He speaks to each child in small, kind words; blesses them, then takes one in his arms and warns his audience, "Whoever does not receive the kingdom of God like a little child will never enter it!"

Christ in My Heart

Lord, what were the qualities
of little children
that you found most endearing?
Was it their happy laughter
and shy waves
as you were passing by their homes?
Their boisterous enthusiasms,
their curiosity about
kittens and caterpillars
and all the wonderful things
of your creation?
Their confident requests
that you fix their toys?
Or was it the trusting way
a child would hold your hand,
or sometimes fall fast asleep
on your shoulder?
At times when I get tired

sorting out the contradictions
of my life
and the complexities of religion,
it's nice to remember
you once said
that the best way to come to you
was with the confidence and love
of those little ones.
Help me, Lord, to act
more like a little child
toward you!

Christ in My Hands

I will pretend less and trust more in my conversation with the Lord.

Reflect

"Whoever does not receive the Kingdom of God like a child will never enter it!"

Private Prisons 20

Christ in My Eyes

When John the Baptist heard in prison about Christ's works, he sent some of his disciples to him. "Tell us," they asked Jesus, "are you the one John said was going to come, or should we expect someone else?"

Jesus answered, "Go back and tell John what you are hearing and seeing: the blind can see, the lame can walk, the lepers are made clean, the deaf hear, the dead are raised to life, and the Good News is preached to the poor. How happy is he who has no doubts about me!" Mt 11:2-6.

The stone wall of an immense prison.

John's disciples and I have crept stealthily through darkened streets and back alleys and we now stand in the shadows tossing pebbles at a barred window in the prison wall. Soon the gaunt, bearded face of John the Baptist peers out of a dark cell and his disciples strain to catch his words. The Baptist's hands grasp the iron bars and he whispers hoarsely that we must find Jesus and deliver a special message: "Are you the one who is going to come, or should we expect someone else?"

Christ in My Heart

I am haunted by that picture
of the Baptist's haggard face
peering out from behind the bars of his cell.
He was a simple man
with a special mission —
prepare the way of the Lord
into the hearts of his people.
But circumstances over which John had no control,
events for which he was not completely responsible,
took away his freedom.
How many of the faces I greet every day
look out at me from private "prisons"
no less real than John's?
Sometimes people put walls around themselves
because of the mistakes of their parents,
the misunderstandings of friends,
or because of personal sins,
but their lives speak to me
with words that sound like John's.
They search my face,
seek my heart,
and ask, "Are you the one who is going to come?"

Who will accept me,
love me,
free me,
"or should we expect someone else?"

Christ in My Hands

Today I will really try to listen to the needs of those around me.

Reflect

"Are you the one who is going to come?"

Crosses 21

Christ in My Eyes

Then the mother of Zebedee's sons came to Jesus with her sons, bowed before him, and asked him for a favor.

"What do you want?" Jesus asked her. She answered, "Promise that these two sons of mine will sit at your right and your left when you are King."

"You don't know what you are asking for," Jesus answered them. "Can you drink the cup that I am about to drink?"

"We can," they answered.

"You will indeed drink from my cup," Jesus told them, "but I do not have the right to choose who will sit at my right and my left. These places belong to those for whom my Father has prepared them." Mt 20:20-23.

A noisy marketplace in a Palestinian village.

Merchants call out their wares from under the awnings of roadside booths, farmers haggle over the price of chickens and goats, while busy shoppers elbow their way through the crowded street. Jesus and I are moving slowly among the throngs when a determined-looking woman plants herself in the Lord's path. It is the mother of James and John who trail along behind. "What do you want?" Jesus asks. The woman clutches at his sleeve. "Promise me," she pleads, "that my two sons will sit at your side when you become a king." "You don't know what you are asking," the Lord answers gravely, then looking at James and John, he queries, "Can you drink the cup that I am about to drink?"

Christ in My Heart

Jesus,
following you has brought me
great contentment and peace.
But today you remind me,
as you reminded James and John,
that discipleship sometimes means
drinking your cup,
sharing in your sufferings.
If I have rejoiced with you in moments of glory,
then I should also expect to stand beside you
on the hill of Calvary.
How do I usually react to
the sudden misfortunes and unexpected setbacks
that occur from time to time
in my life
and in the lives of those whom I love?
Do I try to avoid life's suffering at all cost?
Do I drink your cup only grudgingly?

Or, do I see my crosses as somehow extending
your redemptive work
among the human family?
You offer me your cup, Lord.
Help me
to accept it.

Christ in My Hands

I will freely accept a pressing problem and work to its solution.

Reflect

"The Son of Man . . . did not come to be served, but to serve and give his life to redeem many people."

Perseverance 22

Read the following gospel passage and write your own meditation.

Christ in My Eyes

Then Jesus left and went away to the territory near the city of Tyre. He went into a house, and did not want anyone to know he was there; but he could not stay hidden. A certain woman, whose daughter had an evil spirit in her, heard about Jesus and came to him at once and fell at his feet. The woman was a foreigner, born in Phoenicia of Syria. She begged Jesus to drive the demon out of her daughter. But Jesus answered, "Let us feed the children first; it isn't right to take the children's food and throw it to the dogs."

"Sir," she answered, "even the dogs under the table eat the children's leftovers!"

So Jesus said to her, "For such an answer you may go home; the demon has gone out of your daughter!"

She went back home and found her child lying on the bed; the demon had indeed gone out of her. Mk 7:24-30.

Describe this scene in your own words.

Christ in My Heart

Write a conversation with the Lord based on this gospel.

Christ in My Hands

What is a practical application of this gospel to your daily life?

Reflect

A line from scripture to recall your prayer.

Thankfulness 23

Christ in My Eyes

As Jesus made his way to Jerusalem he went between Samaria and Galilee. He was going into a certain village when he was met by ten lepers. They stood at a distance and shouted, "Jesus! Master! Have pity on us!" Jesus saw them and said to them, "Go and let the priests examine you." On the way they were made clean. One of them, when he saw that he was healed, came back, praising God with a loud voice. He threw himself to the ground at Jesus' feet, thanking him. The man was a Samaritan. Jesus spoke up: "There were ten men made clean; where are the other nine? Why is this foreigner the only one who came back to give thanks to God?" And Jesus said to him, "Get up and go; your faith has made you well." Lk 17:11-19.

We have just been healed. It happened upon meeting Jesus on the road outside the village as we were limping off to show ourselves to the priests. One minute we were covered with blistering sores, the next our skin was clear and clean. The other nine acted like they had suddenly gone mad — shouting and jumping and tearing off their bandages.

I feel whole and alive and very happy. But mostly, I think about God's great gifts. I feel so thankful. So I go back to Jesus, kneel at his feet and, as I hold his hand, try to tell him how grateful I really am. He smiles, but then looks down the road and gently asks, "Where are the other nine?"

Christ in My Heart

Jesus, there is so much in my life
which I take for granted,
so many gifts
for which I never express my thanks—
  the people who care for me,
  starry skies,
  my abilities and talents,
  the love that surrounds me,
  summer sunsets,
  the ways I have been healed and helped to grow,
  the glory of a morning in the spring,
  my family and friends,
  the crossroads I have faced.
For all these and for so many other things,
I just want to say thanks and
tell you again how much
I appreciate your gifts.

Christ in My Hands

I will go out of my way today to thank someone I usually take for granted.

Reflect

"One came back, praising God with a loud voice."

Partings 24

Christ in My Eyes

It was now the day before the Feast of Passover. Jesus knew that his hour had come for him to leave this world and go to the Father. He had always loved those who were his own in the world, and he loved them to the very end . "In a little while you will not see me anymore" [Jesus told them], "and then a little while later you will see me."

Some of his disciples said to the others, "What does this mean? He tells us, 'In a little while you will not see me, and then a little while later you will see me'; and he also says, 'It is because I am going to the Father.' What does this 'a little while' mean?" they asked. "We do not know what he is talking about!"

Jesus knew that they wanted to ask him, so he said to them, "I said, 'In a little while you will not see me, and then a little while later you will see me.' Is this what you are asking about among yourselves? I tell you the truth: you will cry and weep, but the world will be glad; you will be sad, but your sadness will turn into gladness: the kind of gladness that no one can take away from you." Jn 13:1, 16:16-20.

Earlier in the day, Peter and John had followed the man with the water jar back to his home. When they had explained the Lord's request, the owner generously offered the use of a spacious upstairs room where we might gather to celebrate Passover. Peter and John immediately began making preparations for the ritual meal, but the rest of us waited until after sundown before we made our way through back alleys and darkened streets to the site for our supper.

We are now reclining around the table in the upper room. The Lord has washed and dried our feet and, after reclining once more at the table, he begins to share his deepest feelings with us, his friends. The room is very still as Jesus tells us of his love; his voice sounds as if his heart were breaking. Somehow, as I begin to realize that he is saying good-bye and that tonight is the last time we shall be together, I am overwhelmed with a feeling of loneliness and loss. What does he mean that for "a little while" we will not see him?

Christ in My Heart

"A little while," you said, Lord,
to describe our time of parting
and then another "little while"
when we would see you again.
No wonder we ask each other
"What does he mean by this 'little while'?"
From our view of things,
from this side of eternity,
the loss of one we love,
seems so final;
the months and years ahead,
the nights we are alone,
so cold, so silent.

So it helps, in our lonely hours,
when we have lost someone we love —
  a spouse,
  a parent,
  or special friend
to remember the way you view
life's partings,
that it is only just a "little while"
until we see each other once more
and are filled with a gladness
that will never be taken away again.

Christ in My Hands

I will remember someone dear whom I have lost by death and think of the day I will see him or her again.

Reflect

". . . I will see you again. . . ."

Last Requests 25

Christ in My Eyes

For from the Lord I received the teaching that I passed on to you: that the Lord Jesus, on the night he was betrayed, took the bread, gave thanks to God, broke it, and said, "This is my body, which is for you. Do this in memory of me." In the same way, he took the cup after the supper and said, "This cup is God's new covenant, sealed with my blood. Whenever you drink it, do it in memory of me." For until the Lord comes, you proclaim his death whenever you eat this bread and drink from this cup. I Cor 11:23-26.

Once more I find myself in the upper room, reclining at table with Jesus and the apostles. The meal is almost over now and we expect that the Lord will soon give the signal to rise and intone the final prayer. Instead, he takes some unleavened bread in his hands, breaks it into pieces and as he passes it around the table, explains that this bread is his body and that we must do this in his memory. Then he passes a goblet of wine, which is his blood, and again he says that this is the way we should keep his memory.

Christ in My Heart

Lord, if it were the last request
of my mother or father,
or of my best friend,
if they asked that I remember them
in some special way —
   with flowers on their grave,
   or by a yearly visit to a favorite place,
   if they wanted me to preserve their picture
   or complete some unfinished task,
that promise would be gladly kept.
Even a heart as cold as mine
would melt with the love
of such a last request.
Yet here at table,
the night before your death,
you ask that I remember in a certain way:
"Break this bread, drink this cup
and do it in my memory."
But so often I share in your supper,
receive your body and blood,
only when the mood suits me,
or when I have some urgent need.

And even then, like a spoiled child,
I complain about the music,
the sermon or the second collection.
You asked that I remember you
in the breaking of the bread.
Help me to be generous
in keeping your last request.

Christ in My Hands

No matter how I feel next Sunday, I will share in the Lord's Supper as a sign of my love for him.

Reflect

"Do this in memory of me."

26 Betrayals

Christ in My Eyes

They arrested Jesus and took him away into the house of the High Priest; and Peter followed far behind. A fire had been lit in the center of the courtyard, and Peter joined those who were sitting around it. When one of the servant girls saw him sitting there at the fire, she looked straight at him and said, "This man too was with him!" But Peter denied it: "Woman, I don't even know him!" After a little while, a man noticed him and said, "You are one of them, too!" But Peter answered, "Man, I am not!" And about an hour later another man insisted strongly: "There isn't any doubt that this man was with him, because he also is a Galilean!" But Peter answered, "Man, I don't know what you are talking about!" At once, while he was still speaking, a rooster crowed. The Lord turned around and looked straight at Peter, and Peter remembered the Lord's words, how he had said, "Before the rooster crows today, you will say three times that you do not know me." Peter went out and wept bitterly.
Lk 22:54-62.

The inner courtyard of the High Priest's official residence.

Bright stars blink above on a clear, bitterly cold night. Earlier, Peter and I had remained hidden in the garden after the Lord's arrest; then we had followed the distant lanterns as the palace guard led Jesus back to Jerusalem. We were finally able to make our way into the courtyard and began warming ourselves around a fire as Jesus was being arraigned in a nearby building.

We are afraid that we will be recognized, but still want to stay close to the Lord. Twice this evening we have been challenged by servants of the High Priest, but both times Peter swore that we didn't know Jesus. Suddenly another bystander overhears Peter talking to me and, pointing in our direction, loudly insists that we are the Lord's followers. We are frightened by the crowd, so Peter again denies knowing Jesus, "Man, I don't know what you are talking about!" Just then Jesus is led across the courtyard. He turns, looks first at Peter, then he looks at me.

Christ in My Heart

Lord, the sadness in your eyes,
the glance that goes straight to my heart,
tells me what no words
could ever say—
that you expected more of me.
You know this fainthearted follower
is not given to wild enthusiasms
or loud protestations of love.
These you really never asked,
only that I be faithful.
that whenever the moment came
I would acknowledge my love
for you before men.
So I find it hard to look back
into your eyes,

to face my own "betrayals" —
  the too easy compromise of my spiritual ideals,
  my silence when faith is under attack,
  my neglect of religious duties
  for the slightest reason,
  my surrender to the pressures of the group.
Peter left the courtyard,
went out and wept bitterly,
but once realizing his betrayal
learned that love means being faithful.
Forgive my moments of weakness,
strengthen my faintheartedness,
help me to remain loyal to you.

Christ in My Hands

I will be more assertive in defending my personal beliefs when Christian values are under attack.

Reflect

"The Lord turned around and looked straight at Peter, . . ."

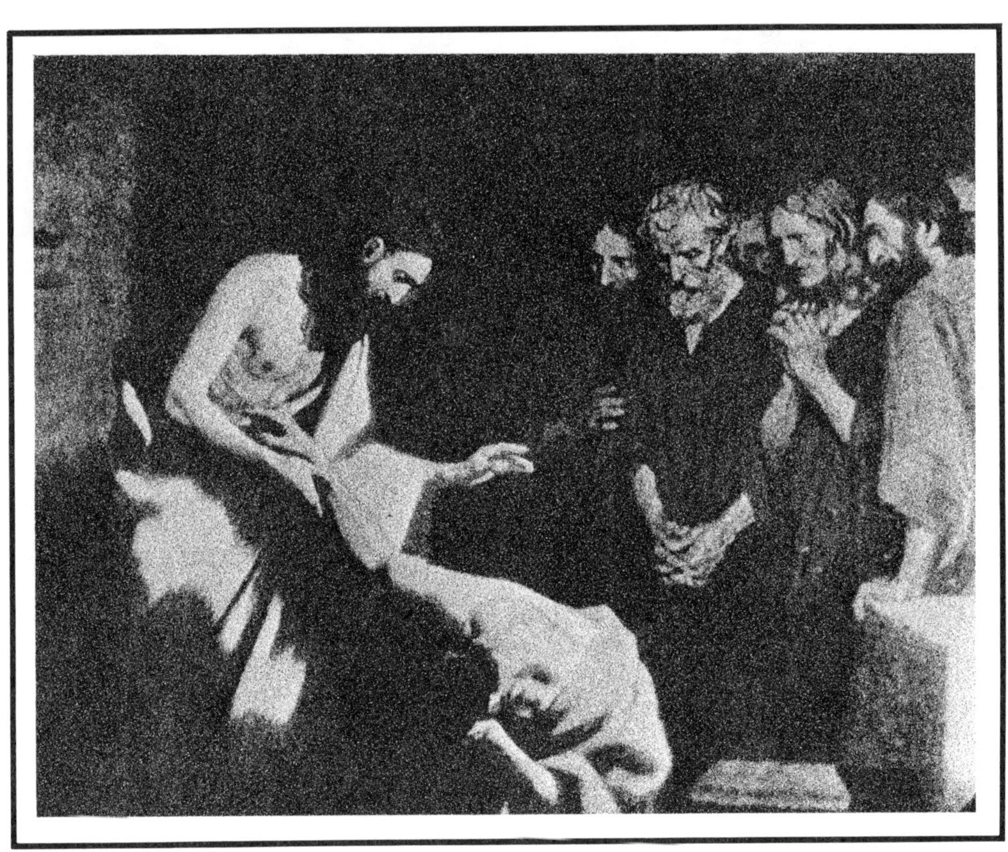

Believing 27

Christ in My Eyes

One of the twelve disciples, Thomas (called the Twin), was not with them when Jesus came. So the other disciples told him, "We saw the Lord!"

Thomas said to them, "If I do not see the scars of the nails in his hands, and put my finger on those scars, and my hand in his side, I will not believe."

A week later the disciples were together indoors again, and Thomas was with them. The doors were locked, but Jesus came and stood among them and said, "Peace be with you." Then he said to Thomas, "Put your finger here, and look at my hands; then stretch out your hand and put it in my side. Stop your doubting, and believe!"

Thomas answered him, "My Lord and my God!"

Jesus said to him, "Do you believe because you see me? How happy are those who believe without seeing me!" Jn 20:24-29.

Just a week ago, Thomas and I had climbed the rickety outside stairs, tapped softly at the barred door and been admitted to the upper room. We were greeted by a group of wild-eyed people, all trying to talk at once, who claimed that Jesus had appeared and spoken to them. Thomas had shaken his head in disbelief, acted like the apostles were religious fanatics and said he would believe their ghost story only when he actually touched the wounds in the hands and side of the Lord.

Tonight we waited until sunset then made our way down the same narrow street and up the familiar stairs to the second-story room. The mood this evening is more subdued, but Thomas and I are greeted warmly. We are just taking our place at table when the room suddenly becomes very still. We glance up to see Jesus standing by the door. He looks much as we remember him and his garments appear the same, but I notice the deep, red wounds in his hands. Jesus offers Thomas those wounded hands and gently chides him for his disbelief. Thomas falls at Jesus' feet and through his tears whispers, "My Lord and my God."

Christ in My Heart

Jesus, I also kneel before you
in the upper room
and confess that I am no better
than the unbelieving apostle.
At least Thomas was honest
about his doubts,
while I claim to be a believer.
But so often I live as if I didn't believe —
   my self-sufficiency,
   my complete preoccupation
   with the here and now,
   the prayers said only in moments of desperate need.
Lord, I do not ask for proof,

only that I may become a believer
without seeing.
I kneel before you,
and with Thomas,
praise you as my Lord and God.
I do believe, Lord,
help my unbelief!

Christ in My Hands

No matter how busy I am today, I will try to lift my heart to the Lord, be aware of his presence and thank him for his gifts.

Reflect

"My Lord and my God."

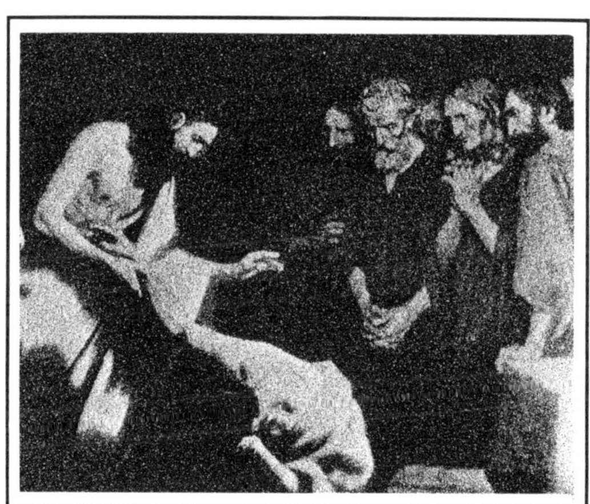

The Breaking of the Bread 28

Christ in My Eyes

That very same day, two of them were on their way to a village called Emmaus, seven miles from Jerusalem, and they were talking together about all that had happened. Now as they talked this over, Jesus himself came up and walked by their side; but something prevented them from recognizing him. He said to them, "What matters are you discussing as you walk along?" They stopped short, their faces downcast.

Then one of them, called Cleopas, answered him, "You must be the only person staying in Jerusalem who does not know the things that have been happening there these last few days." "What things?" he asked. "All about Jesus of Nazareth," they answered, "who proved he was a great prophet by the things he said and did in the sight of God and of the whole people; and how our chief priests and our leaders handed him over to be sentenced to death, and had him crucified. Our own hope had been that he would be the one to set Israel free. And this is not all: two whole days have gone by since it all happened; and some women from our group have astounded us. They went to the tomb in the early morning, and when they did not find the body, they came back to tell us they had seen a vision of angels who declared he was alive. Some of our friends went to the tomb and found everything exactly as the women had reported, but of him they saw nothing."

When they drew near to the village to which they were going, he made as if to go on; but they pressed him to stay with them. "It is nearly evening," they said, "and the day is almost over." So he went in to stay with them. Now while he was with them at table, he took the bread and said the blessing; then he broke it and handed it to them. And their eyes were opened and they recognized him, but he had vanished from their sight. Then they said to each other, "Did not our hearts burn within us as he talked to us on the road and explained the scriptures to us?"
Lk 24:13-24, 28-32 (JB).

A noisy village inn on the Emmaus road where my friend Cleopas and I have stopped for supper.

We are seated at table in a side alcove; sitting across from us is the traveller who had joined us on the road. Somehow his understanding of the scriptures has helped heal the pain in our hearts. The meal is served and we ask our new friend to offer the bread and pronounce the traditional blessing. He breaks the bread in a familiar way and as he is sharing it with us we are stunned to realize that the stranger is Jesus.

Christ in My Heart

Jesus, you remind me elsewhere in scripture
that your flesh is real food,
your blood real drink.
But like the disciples
   on the road to Emmaus,

my eyes aren't accustomed
  to seeing beyond appearances.
How faithfully do I receive the Eucharist?
And even then,
do I not share the bread of heaven
more from the force of habit
than from the fervor of faith?
In the Eucharist you offer healing
for my wounds,
strength for my Christian journey.
Lord, you opened the eyes of those tired travellers,
and they saw you at their meal.
Help me also to recognize you
in the breaking of the bread.

Christ in My Hands

I will prepare myself better for the next time I take Communion.

Reflect

"Did not our hearts burn within us as he talked to us on the road . . .?"

Christ-centering 29

Read the following gospel passage and write your own meditation.

Christ in My Eyes

While they were telling them this, suddenly the Lord himself stood among them and said to them, "Peace be with you."

Full of fear and terror, they thought that they were seeing a ghost. But he said to them, "Why are you troubled? Why are these doubts coming up in your minds? Look at my hands and my feet and see that it is I, myself. Feel me, and you will see, because a ghost doesn't have flesh and bones, as you can see I have."

He said this and showed them his hands and his feet. They still could not believe, they were so full of joy and wonder; so he asked them, "Do you have anything to eat here?" They gave him a piece of cooked fish, which he took and ate before them.

Then he said to them, "These are the very things I told you while I was still with you: everything written about me in the Law of Moses, the writings of the prophets, and the Psalms had to come true." Lk 24:36-44.

Describe this scene in your own words.

Christ in My Heart

Write a conversation with the Lord based on this gospel.

Christ in My Hands

What is a practical application of this gospel to your daily life?

Reflect

A line from scripture to recall your prayer.

Loving 30

Christ in My Eyes

So they went and got into the boat; but all that night they did not catch a thing. As the sun was rising, Jesus stood at the water's edge, but the disciples did not know that it was Jesus. Then he said to them, "Young men, haven't you caught anything?"

"Not a thing," they answered.

He said to them, "Throw your net out on the right side of the boat, and you will find some." So they threw the net out, and could not pull it back in, because they had caught so many fish.

The disciple whom Jesus loved said to Peter, "It is the Lord!" When Simon Peter heard that it was the Lord, he wrapped his outer garment around him (for he had taken his clothes off) and jumped into the water.

Jesus said to Simon Peter, "Simon, son of John, do you love me more than these?"

"Yes, Lord," he answered, "you know that I love you."

Jesus said to him, "Take care of my lambs." A second time Jesus said to him, "Simon, son of John, do you love me?"

"Yes, Lord," he answered, "you know that I love you."

Jesus said to him, "Take care of my sheep." A third time Jesus said, "Simon, son of John, do you love me?"

Peter became sad because Jesus asked him the third time, "Do you love me?" and said to him, "Lord, you know everything; you know that I love you!"

Jesus said to him, "Take care of my sheep." Jn 21:3-8, 15-17.

The lake is mirror-calm and the morning mist is just rising off the waters. I feel the warmth of the sunrise as the new day dawns. My muscles ache from rowing and I hear the lap of water against our little boat. Suddenly, from the shadows along the shore, someone calls. John shields his squinting eyes and then shouts to Peter, "It is the Lord." A moment later the boat rocks as Peter jumps into the water. I follow him, running and splashing up the beach. Suddenly we fall on our knees before Jesus who stands there in his long, white garment. He looks deep into Peter's eyes, and asks him a question. Then he turns to me. The same searching glance as now he calls my name and asks the same question, "Do you love me?"

Christ in My Heart

He calls me by name
and I think of all the reasons I have
for loving him,
the many ways his goodness is shown to me:
  my faith,
  my friends,
  my family,
  my life.
So many gifts despite my mistakes,
my countless failures.
He loves me
and deep down,
I love him, too.
Lord, you know all things,
you know I love you.

Christ in My Hands

Since we take those who are closest so much for granted, I'll say "I love you" the next time I'm with the most important person in my life.

Reflect

"Do you love me?"

Furthering Prayer

Today there is much interest in the "passages," "turning points," "crossings" and the "seasons" of our lives. Growth and change are part of its fabric. So it is with prayer. Our experience of the Lord and the way we communicate with him is a continuing process; it grows through different stages. Here are a few questions most frequently asked by beginners as they encounter their first passages of prayer:

How long should I continue the method of prayer suggested by this book?

As long as you feel yourself growing. Young people, when first learning to ride a two-wheel bike, sometimes use "training wheels" to help them learn and keep them steady. The method of prayer suggested in this book — *Christ in My Eyes, My Heart and My Hands* — is only that, a method. It is designed to support busy people in a hectic world as they take their first steps toward a deeper experience of prayer. If a person faithfully "practices" this method, the day will come — usually within a year or so — when he or she will be able to pray the gospels in his or her own way and own words.

What is the most important value in prayer?

In front of a certain college chapel there is a deep drainage ditch. During the winter months, when drifts of snow cover the highway, unsuspecting drivers sometimes go off the edge of the road into the ditch. A tow truck is called to pull out the car. The important thing for the unlucky driver is the *pull* required to get his or her car back on the road. The kind of equipment used — cable, rope or chain — isn't that significant. So it is with prayer. The thing that unites us to the Lord is *love;* it is the "pull" of our spiritual lives. The form of prayer we employ is secondary as long as we are united to Jesus.

When should a person consider a change in his or her style of prayer?

Around vacation time most men and women usually start noticing the extra pounds acquired over the winter months. Summer sport shirts are a little tight, bathing suits bulge in the wrong places, skirt zippers close with difficulty. So it is really a sign of growth in prayer when our old style of praying doesn't seem to "fit" in exactly the same old way. We have been reasonably faithful to the practice of prayer, have tried to set aside a certain time each day for the Lord, but we begin to feel constrained by our familiar form of prayer. Words become inadequate; talking to the Lord seems to be only that — just words. We hunger for something more, but we don't know what that "something" is. Worse, the Lord himself seems to turn away; he feels "absent." Like a good friend we expected at a party, we are more aware of the Lord because we miss him. We sense the Lord is with us, but he seems to be hidden. Every effort we make to speak to him sounds strained and seems only to put him farther away. Far from becoming discouraged by this experience, or feeling that our prayer is a failure, we should understand these signs as indicators of a "passage," an invitation from the Lord to enter a deeper form of prayer.

What form will this new way of prayer take?

Souls differ more than faces, people grow at their own pace in prayer, so it is difficult to generalize. It is important, however, that we remain faithful to our regular patterns of prayer. We should never abandon our usual time of prayer, for example, simply because we do not seem to be praying.

Many people, at this stage of their spiritual growth, seem drawn to a "prayer of presence." Just as a new mother can wait in silence by her sleeping baby and, without saying anything, be in loving communion with that child, just as a couple can share a sunset without words, so we can be present to the Lord in silent love. Some people begin this type of prayer by reading a passage from scripture and then simply kneeling in the presence of the Lord in loving faith. This, too, is a real form of prayer, but a person who feels drawn to pray this way will usually be helped by seeking the guidance of an experienced spiritual counsellor.

For those interested in furthering prayer, here is a list of self-help books:

Daily We Touch Him, Basil Pennington, O.C.S.O. (Doubleday, 1977) — a practical primer on contemporary and traditional forms of prayer. Everything from Transcendental Meditation to Thomas Merton's "Centering Prayer" explained in an easy, do-it-yourself style.

Difficulties in Mental Prayer, Dom Eugene Boylan (Paulist Press, 1966) — a reprint of a beginner's handbook that has helped a great many Christians grow in prayer. A classic on the ways of prayer for almost forty years.

When the Well Runs Dry, Thomas Green, S.J. (Ave Maria, 1979) — an excellent guide for people who are beginning to experience the "passages of prayer" and feel the need of support and experienced direction.

The Prayer of Faith, Leonard Boase, S.J. (Our Sunday Visitor, 1976) — another reprint of a classic guidebook on the paths of prayer. Very helpful for those with the "I can't pray anymore" feeling.

St. Therese of Lisieux, the Carmelite mystic who died at the age of 24 in 1897, once described her attempts at prayer with a marvelous metaphor. Therese said that spiritually she always felt like a little child who was trying to climb a flight of stairs for the very first time. Her father stood at the top, arms outstretched, calling her to him. By her own efforts, explained Therese, she wasn't even able to put her foot on the first step, let alone climb the whole flight, but she wasn't discouraged. For she was certain that her father loved her, even though she always seemed to fall; and she knew that eventually he would take pity upon her, come down, lift her up in his arms and carry her to the top with him. The Lord loves us no less, said Therese, and if we are reasonably generous in our attempts to pray, he, too, will take pity and bring us close to him.